Lincoln vs. Biden

Johnny Berry

Published by Johnny Berry, 2024.

While every precaution has been taken in the preparation of this book, the publisher assumes no responsibility for errors or omissions, or for damages resulting from the use of the information contained herein.

LINCOLN VS. BIDEN

First edition. December 16, 2024.

ISBN: 979-8230168409

Written by Johnny Berry.

Lincoln vs. Biden

1

Chapter 1: Lincoln's Response to Secession

On the morning of March 4, 1861, Abraham Lincoln stood before the divided nation he had just inherited. His inauguration day was marked by uncertainty, fear, and a dark cloud of looming conflict. By then, seven Southern states had already declared their secession from the Union. South Carolina had led the charge, with Mississippi, Florida, Alabama, Georgia, Louisiana, and Texas following closely behind. The newly formed Confederate States of America, under the leadership of Jefferson Davis, challenged the very foundation of the Union that Lincoln was about to swear to protect. The nation was on the edge of a precipice, and Lincoln's response in these early days would be crucial in shaping the future of the United States.

Lincoln faced an unprecedented crisis. No president before him had ever confronted the dissolution of the Union. Many doubted that he, a self-educated lawyer from the backwoods of Illinois, had the ability to navigate these perilous waters. However, Lincoln's vision was clear: the Union must be preserved at all costs. This vision would drive his decisions throughout the early days of his presidency, informing both his approach to the Southern states and his subsequent actions as the nation slid towards civil war.

Preserving the Union Above All

From the outset, Lincoln's priority was unequivocal—preserving the Union. This goal defined his response to secession, guiding him to avoid rash moves that could further alienate the Southern states that had not yet seceded. In his inaugural address, Lincoln chose a tone of conciliation and reason, rather than one of threats or anger. He extended an olive branch, speaking directly to the Southern people, assuring them that he had no intention to interfere with the institution of slavery where it already existed. He reiterated that his primary duty was to uphold the Constitution, emphasizing that any action against the Union was unlawful.

Lincoln's inaugural address was a masterpiece of careful rhetoric. He balanced firmness with empathy, stressing that secession was not a legally valid option. He famously declared that "in contemplation of universal law and of the Constitution, the Union of these States is perpetual." Lincoln appealed to the shared history and sacrifices that had forged the nation, invoking the "mystic chords of memory" that tied Americans together, North and South. He hoped to remind the Southern states of their common bonds, aiming to dissuade them from the course they had taken without escalating the conflict further.

The Fort Sumter Dilemma

Despite Lincoln's appeals, the situation escalated rapidly. The Confederate states seized federal forts, arsenals, and other properties within their territories, effectively dismantling federal authority in the South. By the time of Lincoln's inauguration, Fort Sumter in Charleston Harbor remained one of the last federal outposts in Confederate territory. It became a symbol of the brewing conflict, a litmus test for Lincoln's resolve.

Lincoln faced a difficult choice: reinforce Fort Sumter and risk war, or abandon it and tacitly acknowledge the legitimacy of secession. Abandoning Fort Sumter would mean conceding to the Confederacy's demands, signaling a dangerous weakness that could embolden other states considering secession. On the other hand, resupplying it could provoke outright war—a reality Lincoln was not eager to initiate, especially as the North was not yet unified in its desire for conflict.

In April 1861, after careful deliberation, Lincoln decided to send a supply ship to the fort, notifying South Carolina's governor that it would deliver only provisions—food, not arms. This move was a calculated one. Lincoln hoped to place the burden of starting a war squarely on the Confederacy, forcing them into a decision: allow the fort to be resupplied or initiate conflict themselves. The Confederates, determined to assert their authority, chose the latter. On April 12, 1861, Confederate forces opened fire on Fort Sumter, marking the start of the Civil War.

Mobilizing the North

Lincoln's response to the attack on Fort Sumter was immediate. He called for 75,000 volunteers to suppress the rebellion—a move that rallied the North but also prompted additional Southern states to secede, including Virginia, Arkansas, Tennessee, and North Carolina. Lincoln understood that to preserve the Union, he would need the full mobilization of the Northern states, not only in manpower but in political will. His call for volunteers demonstrated his commitment to using force, if necessary, to maintain the Union's integrity.

This was a decisive moment for Lincoln. By calling for troops, he was acknowledging that the crisis could no longer be resolved through negotiation alone. The path to preserving the Union now lay through the battlefield. His reluctance to initiate hostilities had been genuine, but once conflict was inevitable, Lincoln showed a resolute determination. He would not allow the Union to crumble under his watch.

Balancing Caution with Action

Throughout these early months, Lincoln walked a fine line between action and restraint. He recognized that aggressive moves could drive the Border States—those slave states that had not seceded—into the Confederacy. Kentucky, Missouri, Maryland, and Delaware were crucial to the Union's strategy; losing them could tip the scales in favor of the Confederacy. To keep these states loyal, Lincoln exercised a careful, sometimes controversial, approach, including suspending habeas corpus in Maryland to prevent secessionist activity and maintain control over this key border state.

Lincoln's strategic patience was often misinterpreted as indecisiveness, but his decisions were driven by a careful assessment of the political landscape. He was willing to make difficult, often unpopular, decisions to hold the Union together. His handling of secession was not about appeasement but about buying time; time to gather support, strengthen the Union's position, and ensure that when conflict came, the North would be ready to fight.

The Moral Turning Point

Initially, Lincoln's approach to secession and the looming conflict was strictly about preserving the Union. However, as the war progressed, Lincoln's thinking began to shift. He started to view the abolition of slavery as intrinsically linked to the survival of the Union. The seeds of emancipation were planted in these early days of the crisis, although it would take another year and the pressing realities of war before Lincoln publicly embraced the cause of ending slavery as a war aim.

Lincoln's evolving vision transformed the Civil War from a struggle to preserve the Union into a fight for a new birth of freedom. His response to secession was not only about holding the country together; it was also about redefining what that Union would stand for in the future. It would be a nation not just united, but also free; a vision that would ultimately lead to the Emancipation Proclamation in 1863.

Summary of Chapter 1

Lincoln's response to secession was marked by a careful blend of diplomacy, restraint, and decisive action. Faced with an unprecedented crisis, he managed to balance the delicate task of preventing further secession while preparing the North for the inevitable conflict. His determination to preserve the Union above all else guided his early presidency, laying the foundation for the struggle that would define his leadership and reshape the United States.

The firing on Fort Sumter was the spark that ignited the Civil War, but Lincoln's steady resolve and strategic foresight ensured that the Union would not be divided without a fight. His early responses to secession set the tone for his leadership—a combination of steadfastness, moral clarity, and an unwavering belief in the promise of the United States. These qualities would carry him through the darkest days of the Civil War, as he worked to keep the nation whole, even as it seemed to be coming apart at the seams.

Chapter 2: The Civil War Begins

The morning of April 12, 1861, brought a thunderous turning point in American history. As Confederate cannons opened fire on Fort Sumter in Charleston Harbor, the delicate balance of diplomacy and restraint that President Abraham Lincoln had sought to maintain shattered irreparably. The bombardment and subsequent surrender of the fort marked not just the start of open conflict but also the beginning of Lincoln's transformation from a cautious statesman into a wartime leader. The preservation of the Union, which had thus far been an abstract ideal, now became a bloody and immediate necessity.

The days and weeks following the attack were a whirlwind of action and decision-making as Lincoln grappled with mobilizing the North, holding the Border States, and confronting the grim reality of civil war.

Rallying the North: A Call to Arms

Fort Sumter's fall electrified the North. Across the Union states, outrage at the Confederate assault on a federal installation sparked a groundswell of patriotism. On April 15, 1861, Lincoln issued a proclamation calling for 75,000 volunteers to serve in state militias for 90 days—a timeline reflecting the widespread but overly optimistic belief that the rebellion could be quelled quickly.

The response to Lincoln's call was overwhelming. Young men from towns and cities rushed to enlist, swelling local militia units with volunteers eager to defend the Union. Churches and civic organizations held rallies to bolster public morale, and newspapers praised Lincoln's resolve.

Yet Lincoln's call to arms was a double-edged sword. While it unified the North, it also drove four more Southern states—Virginia, Arkansas, Tennessee, and North Carolina—into the Confederate fold. Virginia's decision to secede was particularly devastating; not only was it one of the most populous and economically significant states, but it also brought the Confederate capital dangerously close to Washington, D.C. Moreover, its secession cost Lincoln the services of General Robert E. Lee, who chose to side with his home state despite being offered command of Union forces.

Securing the Border States

As Northern enthusiasm surged, Lincoln's administration turned its attention to the critical task of retaining the loyalty of the Border States: Delaware, Maryland, Kentucky, and Missouri. These states, though still part of the Union, were deeply divided in their sympathies, with significant portions of their populations supporting the Confederacy. Losing the Border States would have given the South a substantial strategic advantage, including access to key transportation routes, resources, and manpower.

Lincoln employed a pragmatic, and sometimes heavy-handed, approach to keep these states in the Union. In Maryland, where Confederate sympathies ran high and proximity to Washington made the state critical, Lincoln suspended Habeas Corpus and authorized the arrest of pro-secession legislators. While controversial, these measures prevented Maryland from tipping into rebellion and ensured the capital would not be encircled by hostile forces.

In Kentucky, Lincoln adopted a policy of cautious neutrality. His administration worked behind the scenes to bolster Unionist factions, avoiding actions that might provoke a secessionist backlash. This delicate balance paid off; Kentucky remained in the Union, though it declared itself neutral at the war's outset.

Missouri was a battleground in every sense of the word. Divided loyalties led to skirmishes and guerrilla warfare, requiring Union forces to intervene to stabilize the state. In Delaware, where Confederate sentiment was less pronounced, Lincoln's task was simpler, but he maintained vigilance to ensure the state's loyalty.

The retention of the Border States was a significant achievement for Lincoln's administration. It prevented the Confederacy from expanding its territory and resources and ensured the Union maintained critical geographic advantages.

Building an Army

One of Lincoln's immediate challenges was transforming the Union's unprepared military into a force capable of waging war. In 1861, the United States Army consisted of fewer than 17,000 soldiers, most stationed in scattered outposts along the western frontier. Moreover, a significant number of experienced officers resigned their commissions to join the Confederacy, leaving the Union with a leadership vacuum.

Lincoln appointed General Winfield Scott, a hero of the Mexican-American War, as general-in-chief of the Union Army. Scott's "Anaconda Plan," a strategy to blockade Southern ports and control the Mississippi River, aimed to suffocate the Confederacy economically. While sound in principle, the plan's long-term nature clashed with the public and political demand for swift action.

The Union Army's first major test came in July 1861 at the First Battle of Bull Run (Manassas), where Lincoln's pressure for a quick offensive resulted in a poorly coordinated and disastrous defeat. The loss was a sobering reminder that the war would be neither short nor easy. In response, Lincoln redoubled his efforts to build a professional army, signing legislation to expand troop enlistments and federalize state militias.

Managing Public Opinion

Lincoln understood that maintaining public support was as critical as military success. The press played a powerful role in shaping perceptions of the war, and Lincoln worked to cultivate favorable coverage. He gave interviews to influential editors, penned anonymous editorials, and maintained an open line of communication with newspaper publishers.

Despite these efforts, Lincoln faced criticism from both ends of the political spectrum. Radical Republicans criticized him for not taking a stronger stance against slavery, while Democrats accused him of violating civil liberties and overstepping his constitutional authority. Lincoln's ability to navigate these tensions without alienating key constituencies was a testament to his political skill.

The Weight of Wartime Leadership

The outbreak of war placed unprecedented demands on Lincoln. He assumed powers that no previous president had wielded, including the suspension of habeas corpus and the expansion of the military without prior congressional approval. These actions, while controversial, were justified by Lincoln as necessary to preserve the Union. His leadership in these early months set the tone for the war: pragmatic, decisive, and deeply focused on the ultimate goal of national unity.

For Lincoln, the stakes of the war extended beyond territorial integrity. He viewed the conflict as a test of the American experiment in democracy. If the Union could not survive internal rebellion, it would send a dangerous signal to the world that self-government was inherently unstable.

Summary of Chapter 2

The early months of the Civil War were marked by rapid and difficult decisions that tested Lincoln's leadership and the resilience of the nation. From the rallying of volunteers to the strategic importance of the Border States, Lincoln navigated a complex and evolving crisis with a clear-eyed focus on preserving the Union. The fall of Fort Sumter had plunged the nation into war, but it was Lincoln's resolve that ensured the Union would not collapse under the weight of its divisions.

The Civil War's beginnings revealed both the fragility and strength of the United States. For Lincoln, these early challenges were only the start of a long and arduous journey. The Union's survival depended not only on military victory but on his ability to hold together a divided populace and inspire the nation to endure the trials ahead.

Chapter 3: The Conclusion of the War

By the spring of 1865, four years of bloodshed and sacrifice had brought the Civil War to its decisive climax. The Union, under President Abraham Lincoln's unyielding leadership, had weathered early defeats, political divisions, and massive casualties to emerge victorious. The war's end was not merely a military conclusion but a turning point that redefined the nation's identity and set the stage for Reconstruction. Yet, as Union forces celebrated triumph on the battlefield, Lincoln knew the greater challenge lay ahead: binding the nation's wounds and charting a new course for a country transformed by war.

The Final Campaigns

The final months of the Civil War saw Union forces execute the strategies that had been years in the making. General Ulysses S. Grant, whom Lincoln had entrusted with overall command in 1864, pursued a relentless campaign against Robert E. Lee's Army of Northern Virginia. Grant's strategy of attrition sought to exhaust the Confederacy's resources and resolve. Meanwhile, General William Tecumseh Sherman's devastating March to the Sea further crippled the South's infrastructure and morale, cutting a path of destruction from Atlanta to Savannah.

The culmination of these efforts came in April 1865, when Lee's forces, weakened and surrounded, abandoned Richmond and retreated westward. On April 9, 1865, Lee surrendered to Grant at Appomattox Court House in Virginia. The event was marked by Grant's magnanimity; his terms of surrender were designed to promote reconciliation, allowing Confederate soldiers to return home with their horses and personal belongings. Grant's approach mirrored Lincoln's desire to reunify the nation with minimal recrimination.

Despite Lee's surrender, sporadic resistance continued in other parts of the South. Confederate General Edmund Kirby Smith, commanding forces west of the Mississippi River, held out for weeks, refusing to concede. In an ironic twist of fate, the last official battle of the Civil War occurred after Lee's surrender. On May 12–13, 1865, Union and Confederate forces clashed at the Battle of Palmito Ranch near Brownsville, Texas. Despite being a Confederate victory, the battle had no strategic impact, as the war was already over in all but name.

General Granger's March to Galveston

Even after Lee's surrender, word of the Union's victory and the emancipation of enslaved people spread slowly, particularly in the more remote corners of the Confederacy. Texas, isolated by distance and geography, became a final holdout of Confederate defiance. Slavery persisted in the state despite the Emancipation Proclamation of 1863 and Lee's capitulation in April 1865.

It was not until June 19, 1865, when Union General Gordon Granger and his forces arrived in Galveston, Texas, that the war's final chapter began to close. Standing before a gathering of residents, Granger read General Order No. 3, which announced the emancipation of enslaved people in Texas. This moment, now celebrated annually as Juneteenth, marked a pivotal step in the Union's efforts to enforce the liberation of millions of formerly enslaved individuals. Granger's arrival symbolized the Union's commitment to ensuring that the promises of freedom and victory extended even to the furthest reaches of the Confederacy.

The Human and Economic Cost

The Civil War exacted a staggering toll on the nation. Over 620,000 soldiers died, making it the deadliest conflict in American history. Civilians, too, bore immense suffering, particularly in the South, where entire cities were reduced to rubble, and the economy was devastated. Enslaved people, numbering approximately four million, emerged from the war free but faced an uncertain future in a society still steeped in racism and economic inequality.

Lincoln was acutely aware of these challenges. In his second inaugural address, delivered just weeks before the war's end, he acknowledged the profound suffering on both sides. His famous words, "With malice toward none, with charity for all," reflected his vision for healing the nation. Yet, even as he called for reconciliation, Lincoln understood the need for accountability and justice, particularly regarding the issue of slavery.

The Thirteenth Amendment: A New Birth of Freedom

The conclusion of war marked the fulfillment of one of Lincoln's most transformative legacies: the abolition of slavery. While the Emancipation Proclamation of 1863 had declared enslaved people in Confederate-held territories free, its legal authority rested on Lincoln's wartime powers. To ensure the permanent abolition of slavery, Lincoln championed the passage of the Thirteenth Amendment to the Constitution.

In January 1865, after intense lobbying by Lincoln and his allies, Congress passed the amendment, which abolished slavery throughout the United States. Ratified later that year, the Thirteenth Amendment represented a monumental shift in the nation's legal and moral foundation. For Lincoln, it was the culmination of his belief that the Union's preservation was inseparable from the elimination of slavery.

The amendment's passage was also a testament to Lincoln's political acumen. He used the full weight of his presidency to rally support, offering political appointments and appealing to the moral convictions of undecided congressmen. His efforts reflected his conviction that the Union's survival depended not only on military victory but also on redefining its principles to include freedom and equality.

Lincoln's Assassination and Its Impact

Tragically, Lincoln did not live to see the full fruits of his labor. On the evening of April 14, 1865, just days after Lee's surrender, Lincoln was shot by John Wilkes Booth while attending a play at Ford's Theatre in Washington, D.C. He died the following morning, plunging the nation into mourning.

Lincoln's assassination shocked the country and left a profound void in its leadership. The task of Reconstruction fell to his successor, Andrew Johnson, a Southern Democrat whose lenient policies toward the former Confederacy would sow division and hinder the progress of Lincoln's vision.

For many, Lincoln's death symbolized the ultimate sacrifice for the Union. He had steered the nation through its darkest hour, preserving its integrity and laying the groundwork for a new era. Yet his absence during Reconstruction left critical questions unanswered: How would the Union treat the defeated South? What role would freed African Americans play in the nation's future? And how could the scars of war be healed in a society still deeply divided?

The War's Legacy

The conclusion of the Civil War marked the beginning of a new chapter in American history. The Union had been preserved, but the nature of that Union had been fundamentally altered. The war had resolved the question of whether states could secede, affirming the supremacy of the federal government. It had also begun the arduous process of dismantling the institution of slavery, though true equality remained far from realized.

As the nation turned to Reconstruction, the challenges were immense. The South lay in ruins, both physically and economically, and the federal government faced the daunting task of reintegrating rebellious states while ensuring justice for freed people. For Lincoln, the war's end was an opportunity to redefine the nation's principles, extending the promise of liberty and democracy to all Americans. Though his life was cut short, his vision would endure, shaping the course of Reconstruction and the constitutional amendments that followed.

Summary of Chapter 3

The Civil War's conclusion brought both relief and uncertainty. The Union had survived its greatest test, and slavery had been abolished, but the work of rebuilding the nation was just beginning. Lincoln's leadership during the war had set the stage for a new era, but his assassination left the task of realizing his vision to others.

In the months and years that followed, the United States would grapple with the meaning of freedom and equality. The Reconstruction Amendments—the Thirteenth, Fourteenth, and Fifteenth—would form the backbone of this effort, seeking to address the war's causes and consequences. Yet the path forward would be fraught with conflict and resistance, as the nation struggled to reconcile its ideals with its realities.

As the dust of war settled, the question loomed: Could the Union truly heal, and could its promises of liberty and justice be extended to all? The answers lay in the Reconstruction era, where the battle for the soul of the nation would continue.

Chapter 4: The Reconstruction Constitutional Amendments

The Civil War ended with the Union preserved, but the nation faced profound questions about how to reconstruct a society that had been built on the institution of slavery. The task was monumental: the South lay in ruins, four million formerly enslaved people were now free, and the country was deeply divided over how to achieve justice and equality.

The Reconstruction Era (1865–1877) was a time of both hope and conflict, and its legacy would be enshrined in three landmark amendments to the U.S. Constitution: the Thirteenth, Fourteenth, and Fifteenth. These amendments, collectively known as the Reconstruction Amendments, were designed to address the causes and consequences of the Civil War and to create a new foundation for the United States as a nation of liberty and equality. However, their implementation and enforcement would be contested every step of the way.

The Thirteenth Amendment: Ending Slavery

The first and most immediate task of Reconstruction was to abolish slavery across the United States. While Lincoln's Emancipation Proclamation in 1863 had declared enslaved people in Confederate-controlled areas free, it did not apply to Union-held slave states like Kentucky and Delaware or have the permanence of constitutional law.

The Thirteenth Amendment, passed by Congress on January 31, 1865, and ratified on December 6, 1865, declared:

"Neither slavery nor involuntary servitude, except as a punishment for crime whereof the party shall have been duly convicted, shall exist within the United States, or any place subject to their jurisdiction."

This amendment was a watershed moment in American history, abolishing slavery nationwide and freeing millions of African Americans. Yet its significance extended beyond emancipation. The amendment also gave Congress the authority to pass legislation to enforce its provisions, laying the groundwork for laws aimed at dismantling the remnants of slavery, such as the Black Codes enacted by Southern states to limit the rights of freed people.

Despite its monumental achievement, the Thirteenth Amendment faced challenges. Southern states resisted its implications, enacting policies to maintain white supremacy and exploit the labor of African Americans through systems like sharecropping and convict leasing. The amendment ended slavery as a legal institution but left unresolved the question of what freedom would mean in practice.

The Fourteenth Amendment: Citizenship and Equal Protection

As the Union sought to reconstruct the South and integrate freed people into American society, it became clear that additional constitutional measures were necessary to define and protect the rights of African Americans. The Fourteenth Amendment, ratified on July 9, 1868, addressed these issues head-on.

The amendment's key provisions included:

1. **Citizenship Clause**: Declared that all persons born or naturalized in the United States were citizens, overturning the Dred Scott decision of 1857, which had denied citizenship to African Americans.
2. **Equal Protection Clause**: Prohibited states from denying any person within their jurisdiction the equal protection of the laws.
3. **Due Process Clause**: Prevented states from depriving any person of life, liberty, or property without due process of law.
4. **Disqualification of Insurrectionists**: Section 3 of the amendment barred individuals who had engaged in rebellion or insurrection from holding public office unless Congress removed the disqualification.

The Fourteenth Amendment fundamentally redefined the relationship between the federal government and the states, asserting federal authority to protect individual rights. It also laid the foundation for future civil rights movements, as the Equal Protection Clause would become a cornerstone of legal challenges to segregation, discrimination, and other injustices.

However, the Fourteenth Amendment's Equal Protection Clause did not extend to women. The amendment explicitly included the word "male" in Section 2, which addressed representation and voting rights, marking the first time the Constitution explicitly referenced gender. Women's rights activists, who had hoped that the promises of equality would encompass all citizens, felt betrayed by this exclusion. Leaders like Elizabeth Cady Stanton and Susan B. Anthony campaigned for women's suffrage and condemned the prioritization of male suffrage in the Fifteenth Amendment.

The exclusion of women highlighted the limits of the Reconstruction Amendments. While they sought to redefine American democracy by addressing race, they left gender inequality unchallenged, reinforcing the societal norms that confined women's political and legal status.

The Fifteenth Amendment: Securing the Right to Vote

The final Reconstruction amendment aimed to secure political participation for African Americans, particularly Black men. The Fifteenth Amendment, ratified on February 3, 1870, declared:

"The right of citizens of the United States to vote shall not be denied or abridged by the United States or by any State on account of race, color, or previous condition of servitude."

The amendment represented a bold step toward racial equality, granting African American men the constitutional right to vote. During the early years of Reconstruction, this promise was realized as Black men voted in large numbers, held public office, and played a vital role in reshaping Southern governments.

However, the Fifteenth Amendment did not extend suffrage to women, a deliberate omission that created a rift within the broader movement for equality. Stanton, Anthony, and others in the women's suffrage movement criticized the amendment for codifying the exclusion of women, arguing that it perpetuated gender-based discrimination. This division underscored the competing priorities within Reconstruction and the difficulty of achieving a unified vision of equality.

Challenges to Enforcement

While the Reconstruction Amendments were groundbreaking, their enforcement depended on the political will of Congress, the president, and the courts. During the early years of Reconstruction, Radical Republicans in Congress passed legislation to protect African Americans' rights, including the Civil Rights Act of 1866 and the Enforcement Acts, which targeted voter suppression and racial violence.

However, as Reconstruction progressed, political opposition to these measures grew. The presidency of Andrew Johnson, who succeeded Lincoln, was marked by leniency toward the South and vetoes of key civil rights legislation. Though Congress overrode many of Johnson's vetoes, his resistance weakened the federal government's commitment to Reconstruction.

The Supreme Court also played a role in undermining the Reconstruction Amendments. Decisions like *The Slaughter-House Cases* (1873) and *United States v. Cruikshank* (1876) narrowly interpreted the Fourteenth and Fifteenth Amendments, limiting their ability to protect African Americans from state-sponsored discrimination and violence.

Legacy of the Reconstruction Amendments

Despite the challenges of enforcement, the Reconstruction Amendments transformed the Constitution and laid the foundation for the ongoing struggle for civil rights. They established the principle that equality under the law was a fundamental American value and provided the legal tools that would later be used to challenge segregation, disenfranchisement, and systemic racism.

The exclusion of women from the full benefits of these amendments, however, served as a stark reminder of the limits of 19th-century reform. Women's suffrage would not be realized until the passage of the Nineteenth Amendment in 1920, after decades of persistent activism. This omission demonstrated that Reconstruction, while revolutionary, was incomplete in its promise of equality.

Summary of Chapter 4

The Reconstruction Amendments were born out of the ashes of the Civil War, representing a bold effort to address the war's root causes and consequences. They abolished slavery, defined citizenship, and guaranteed the right to vote, transforming the Constitution into a document that aspired to fulfill the ideals of liberty and equality for all. Yet their implementation and enforcement would be fraught with resistance, highlighting the enduring tension between America's ideals and its realities.

By excluding women from their guarantees, the amendments reflected the priorities and limitations of their time. Nevertheless, they provided the foundation for future movements for equality, reminding generations of Americans that the fight for justice is a continuous process.

Chapter 5: The Application of Section 3 of the 14th Amendment

The Reconstruction amendments were crafted in the wake of the Civil War to rebuild a fractured nation while safeguarding its democratic principles. Among these, Section 3 of the 14th Amendment sought to address the critical issue of political accountability. By disqualifying individuals who had engaged in insurrection or rebellion, or given aid or comfort to such actions, from holding public office, Section 3 aimed to ensure that the very fabric of the Union would not be endangered by those who betrayed it.

The text of Section 3 reads as follows:

"No person shall be a Senator or Representative in Congress, or elector of President and Vice President, or hold any office, civil or military, under the United States, or under any State, who, having previously taken an oath, as a member of Congress, or as an officer of the United States, or as a member of any State legislature, or as an executive or judicial officer of any State, to support the Constitution of the United States, shall have engaged in insurrection or rebellion against the same, or given aid or comfort to the enemies thereof. But Congress may, by a vote of two-thirds of each House, remove such disability."

The interpretation and enforcement of Section 3 have long been subjects of debate, but recent events surrounding the January 6, 2021, insurrection have brought these questions to the forefront. Central to this discussion is the nature of Section 3 itself, its constitutional enforcement mechanisms, and the actions—or inaction—of President Joe Biden and other institutions in the wake of these events.

The Self-Executing Nature of Section 3

My position is that Section 3 of the 14th Amendment is self-executing. This means that the disqualification prescribed by Section 3 is automatically invoked by an individual's engagement in insurrection or rebellion, or by their provision of aid or comfort to those actions. No additional legislative or judicial action is necessary to activate the disqualification; the provision applies solely based on the conduct of the individual.

From this perspective, courts, whether state or federal, including the Supreme Court, have only a narrow jurisdiction under Section 3. Courts can determine two essential questions:

1. **Did an insurrection or rebellion occur?**
2. **Did the individual in question participate in or give aid or comfort to that insurrection?**

If a court finds that an insurrection occurred and that the individual did not participate in it, Section 3 does not apply. Conversely, if the court determines that an insurrection occurred and that the individual participated in it, the disqualification is automatic, and the court's jurisdiction ends. At this point, the only constitutional remedy is for Congress, by a two-thirds vote in both houses, to remove the disability. Courts do not have the authority to invoke the disqualification or dismiss it, as these powers are explicitly reserved to Congress.

This interpretation underscores the rigid structure of Section 3: accountability is triggered by action (engagement in insurrection), and the remedy is strictly confined to Congress's constitutional authority.

President Biden's Constitutional Obligations

Given the self-executing nature of Section 3, my position asserts that President Biden is constitutionally duty-bound to ensure its enforcement. As chief executive, his oath of office requires him to "take care that the laws be faithfully executed," which includes constitutional provisions like Section 3. In light of **H. Res. 24 (117th Congress),** the article of impeachment passed by the House of Representatives stating that former President Donald Trump incited an insurrection—President

Biden arguably had sufficient grounds to enforce Section 3 against Trump and potentially other members of Congress.

However, President Biden's approach following January 6, 2021, reflects a deliberate choice to avoid invoking Section 3. By framing his presidency as an opportunity for voters to choose between constitutional democracy and authoritarianism, Biden deferred accountability to the electoral process. While this decision may have been motivated by political considerations or a desire to foster unity, my position is that it violated his oath of office. Inaction of enforcing Section 3 allowed individuals who participated in or supported the insurrection to continue serving in government, undermining the very constitutional safeguards designed to protect the nation from such threats.

The Role of the Supreme Court and Other Institutions

The Supreme Court's refusal to address whether January 6 constituted an insurrection, or to evaluate the participation of Trump and other officials in that insurrection, has left critical questions unanswered. This judicial inaction has further weakened the enforcement of Section 3, effectively placing the burden of accountability on Congress and the executive branch.

From my perspective, the Court's reluctance to engage with Section 3 violates its constitutional duty to interpret and uphold the law. While courts lack the authority to dismiss or impose disqualification under Section 3, they do have jurisdiction to establish whether an insurrection occurred and whether specific individuals participated in it. By declining to hear such cases, the judiciary has abdicated its responsibility to clarify the application of this constitutional provision.

Comparing Biden's Inaction to Trump's and Congressional Republicans' Actions

In my view, President Biden's decision to defer enforcement of Section 3 contrasts sharply with the actions of former President Trump and Republican members of Congress leading up to, on, and after January 6. While Trump and his allies engaged in a concerted effort to undermine the 2020 election results—including propagating baseless claims of fraud, pressuring state officials, and encouraging supporters to march on the Capitol—Biden's inaction allowed these individuals to escape constitutional accountability.

The failure to enforce Section 3 has had significant consequences:

- Members of Congress who supported the insurrection, whether through direct participation or rhetorical support, remain in positions of power, creating a dangerous precedent.
- Trump, who has publicly stated his willingness to terminate the Constitution, is now the president-elect, threatening the principles of constitutional governance.
- The Republican Party's alignment with Trump's authoritarian agenda, coupled with convincing evidence that some members would support constitutional termination, underscores the urgency of enforcing Section 3.

The Constitutional Duty to Enforce Section 3

My position further argues that President Biden is constitutionally obligated to prevent the transfer of power to a president-elect who has stated an intent to terminate the Constitution. If Section 3 applies to such an individual, Biden has a duty to enforce it, as allowing the transfer of power would constitute a direct violation of his oath to "preserve, protect, and defend the Constitution of the United States."

This duty extends beyond Trump to Republican members of Congress who have demonstrated loyalty to Trump over the Constitution. By failing to address these threats, Biden risks enabling the erosion of constitutional democracy and the establishment of an authoritarian regime.

Summary of Chapter 5

Section 3 of the 14th Amendment is a powerful yet underutilized tool for protecting the Constitution against those who would betray it.

Its self-executing nature imposes a clear and automatic disqualification on individuals who engage in insurrection, leaving Congress as the sole body empowered to remove this disability. Courts have a limited role in determining the facts of an insurrection and an individual's participation but cannot dismiss or enforce the disqualification.

President Biden's decision to rely on the electoral process rather than enforcing Section 3 represents a significant departure from his constitutional obligations. While motivated by political considerations, this inaction has allowed insurrectionists and their allies to remain in positions of power, undermining the principles of accountability and justice.

The application of Section 3 is not merely a historical question but a pressing issue for the future of American democracy. As threats to the Constitution persist, the failure to enforce its provisions risk enabling the very authoritarianism Section 3 was designed to prevent.

Chapter 6: The Insurrection of 2020—Background and Build-Up

The events of January 6, 2021, shocked the nation and the world. A violent mob stormed the U.S. Capitol in an unprecedented attack on the heart of American democracy, seeking to overturn the results of a free and fair presidential election. This assault was not a spontaneous outburst of anger but the culmination of months, if not years, of rhetoric and actions designed to undermine confidence in democratic institutions and erode the public's trust in electoral processes.

To fully understand the constitutional crisis President Joe Biden inherited, it is essential to examine the background and build-up to the 2020 insurrection, including the roles played by key actors, the dissemination of misinformation, and the systemic failures that allowed these events to unfold.

The Precursor: Trump's Authoritarian Playbook

The seeds of the January 6 insurrection were sown well before the 2020 election. Donald Trump's presidency was marked by a disregard for democratic norms and an embrace of authoritarian tactics. He repeatedly questioned the legitimacy of elections, even claiming—without evidence—that millions of votes were cast illegally in the 2016 election, which he won. This baseless rhetoric set the stage for his broader assault on democratic institutions.

In the lead-up to the 2020 election, Trump amplified these claims. He attacked mail-in voting, a critical option during the COVID-19 pandemic, as inherently fraudulent, despite no evidence supporting such assertions. He also refused to commit to a peaceful transfer of power if he lost, raising alarm about his intentions.

As Election Day approached, Trump and his allies laid the groundwork for what they called a "red mirage," a scenario where early, in-person voting would favor Republicans while later counts of mail-in ballots would swing to Democrats. Trump preemptively declared that any shift in vote totals after Election Night would be proof of fraud, a claim contradicted by the standard processes of election administration.

The "Big Lie" and Its Spread

After Joe Biden was declared the winner of the 2020 election, Trump refused to concede, instead promoting what came to be known as the "Big Lie"—the baseless assertion that the election had been "stolen" through widespread fraud. This claim was debunked by multiple audits, recounts, and court rulings across several states, including those led by Republican officials. Nevertheless, Trump's relentless repetition of the falsehood convinced a significant portion of his supporters that the election results were illegitimate.

Key allies played critical roles in spreading the Big Lie:

1. **Media Amplification**: Conservative media outlets, particularly certain personalities on Fox News, OANN, and Newsmax, amplified Trump's claims, reaching millions of viewers.

2. **Legal Challenges**: Figures like Rudy Giuliani and Sidney Powell spearheaded a series of lawsuits challenging the election results. Although these cases were overwhelmingly dismissed for lack of evidence, they created a narrative of ongoing legal battles that fueled public doubt.

3. **Elected Officials**: Over 100 Republican members of Congress either voiced support for Trump's claims or declined to refute them, lending institutional credibility to the Big Lie.

Pressure Campaigns and Planning the "Nonviolent Coup"

Beyond public rhetoric, Trump and his allies engaged in coordinated efforts to overturn the election results through both legal and extralegal means. Key elements of this campaign included:

1. **State-Level Pressure**: Trump personally pressured state officials to "find" votes or decertify results, as seen in his infamous call to Georgia Secretary of State Brad Raffensperger.
2. **Alternate Electors Scheme**: Allies developed plans to submit slates of pro-Trump electors from states won by Biden, hoping to create confusion during the Electoral College certification process.
3. **Department of Justice Interference**: Trump attempted to enlist the Justice Department in his efforts, even considering the appointment of Jeffrey Clark, who was willing to push baseless claims of fraud. In Trump v. United States, the Supreme Court ruled that the conversations between Trump and the acting Attorney General Jeffrey Clark aimed at claiming the 2020 election had enough fraud to change the outcome of the election, was an official act in Trump's capacity as President of the United States, and therefore could not be used as evidence in a criminal case against him.
4. **Peter Navarro's "Green Bay Sweep"**: Navarro openly described a plan to use congressional allies to delay certification of the Electoral College, creating an opportunity for state legislatures to intervene and reverse Biden's victory. Though labeled a "nonviolent coup," it represented a direct attack on democratic processes and it is probably not cover under the Speech and Debate Clause in the Constitution, that shields members of Congress from prosecution related to their official capacity as legislators.

The Role of January 6

The final step in this effort was the January 6, 2021, joint session of Congress to certify the Electoral College results. Trump and his allies framed this day as a last chance to "stop the steal," urging Vice President

Mike Pence to reject the certification—an action Pence rightly argued was beyond his constitutional authority.

Trump's rally on the morning of January 6 further inflamed tensions. Addressing a crowd of supporters near the White House, he repeated the Big Lie and urged them to "fight like hell." Members of the crowd, many armed and openly planning violence, marched to the Capitol, where the certification process was underway. What followed was a coordinated assault on the Capitol, including violent clashes with law enforcement, vandalism, and attempts to locate and harm elected officials.

Failures of Preparedness and Response

The insurrection revealed systemic failures in law enforcement and security:

- **Intelligence Warnings Ignored**: Multiple reports indicated that far-right groups were planning violence on January 6, yet federal agencies failed to adequately prepare.
- **Delayed National Guard Deployment**: Bureaucratic obstacles and resistance from the Trump administration delayed the National Guard's response, leaving Capitol police overwhelmed.
- **Internal Sabotage**: Reports suggest that key Trump allies within the administration resisted efforts to secure the Capitol, compounding the chaos.

Aftermath and Continuing Threats

The insurrection marked the most direct assault on American democracy since the Civil War, but its aftermath revealed the depth of the ongoing threat:

- **Institutional Impunity**: While hundreds of rioters have been prosecuted, accountability for political leaders who incited or supported the attack remains elusive.

- **Persistence of the Big Lie**: Polls show that a significant portion of Republican voters continue to believe the 2020 election was stolen, undermining trust in future elections.
- **Erosion of Democratic Norms**: Republican legislatures in key states have passed laws restricting voting access and increasing partisan control over election administration, echoing the tactics that enabled the insurrection.

Summary of Chapter 6

The insurrection of 2020 was not an isolated event but the culmination of a sustained effort to subvert American democracy. Its roots lie in the deliberate undermining of electoral integrity, the erosion of institutional safeguards, and the willingness of political actors to prioritize loyalty to a leader over the Constitution.

As the nation reflects on these events, the challenge remains: how to address the forces that enabled the insurrection and prevent such a crisis from recurring. With this context established, the next chapter will turn to a comparison of how Lincoln and Biden navigated their respective constitutional crises, exploring the parallels and divergences in their approaches to leadership, accountability, and the preservation of democracy.

Chapter 7: Biden's Response to the Insurrection

When Joe Biden assumed the presidency on January 20, 2021, he inherited a nation deeply shaken by the violent events of January 6. The attack on the Capitol, a direct attempt to overturn the 2020 presidential election results, was a defining moment in modern American history. It exposed not only the fragility of democratic institutions but also the persistence of forces willing to undermine them for political power.

Biden's response to this constitutional crisis was shaped by his commitment to unity, his respect for the rule of law, and his strategic calculation that the American people should decide the future of democracy through elections. However, his approach has drawn both praise and criticism, particularly regarding his reluctance to invoke constitutional mechanisms like Section 3 of the 14th Amendment.

Condemnation and Inaugural Vision

In his inaugural address, President Biden forcefully condemned the January 6 attack as an assault on democracy, calling it "an unprecedented attack on our democracy." He pledged to restore the soul of the nation, emphasizing the need for unity, healing, and a return to civility in political discourse.

Biden framed his presidency as a moment of renewal, seeking to repair the divisions that had fueled the insurrection. His focus was on restoring faith in democratic institutions, not through punitive measures against his political opponents but by demonstrating that the democratic system could deliver results for all Americans.

This emphasis on unity shaped his broader response to the crisis. Rather than pursue aggressive legal or constitutional action against those responsible for the insurrection, Biden deferred to the judicial system, congressional investigations, and the electoral process to hold individuals accountable.

Deference to the Rule of Law

Biden made it clear early in his presidency that he would not interfere with the Department of Justice's investigations into January 6 or related matters. This commitment to the independence of the judiciary and law enforcement reflected his broader belief in the rule of law as a cornerstone of democracy.

Attorney General Merrick Garland, appointed by Biden, prioritized prosecutions of individuals involved in the Capitol attack. Hundreds of rioters were arrested and charged, with many facing significant prison sentences. However, the DOJ's focus on direct participants in the violence left broader questions of accountability for political leaders largely unaddressed.

Critics argue that Biden's hands-off approach, while respecting institutional norms, missed an opportunity to confront the root causes of the insurrection. By allowing the judicial process to play out without direct intervention, Biden avoided the appearance of politicizing justice but left key figures—including former President Donald Trump and Republican members of Congress who supported the Big Lie—outside the scope of meaningful accountability.

Refraining from Invoking Section 3

Perhaps the most contentious aspect of Biden's response to the insurrection is his decision not to enforce Section 3 of the 14th Amendment, which disqualifies individuals who have engaged in insurrection from holding public office.

Arguments for Enforcement: The January 6 attack, combined with **H. Res. 24 (117th Congress)**—the House's impeachment article accusing Trump of inciting insurrection—provided ample grounds to invoke Section 3 against Trump and other officials. Biden, as the chief executive, had a constitutional duty to "take care that the laws be faithfully executed," which could have included directing federal agencies to assess and enforce Section 3 where applicable.

Arguments Against Enforcement: Biden's decision not to invoke Section 3 appears rooted in his desire to avoid exacerbating political divisions. By framing his presidency as a chance for Americans to choose between democracy and authoritarianism through future elections, Biden sought to depoliticize the question of accountability and allow voters to serve as the ultimate arbiters of justice.

While this strategy may have been well-intentioned, critics contend that it undermined the Constitution's self-executing provisions. Allowing individuals who participated in or supported the insurrection to remain in power, or to seek future office, has emboldened anti-democratic forces and normalized attacks on constitutional governance.

Biden's Focus on Unity and Democracy

Biden's emphasis on unity and restoring faith in democracy has been a central theme of his presidency. He has consistently argued that the best way to counter authoritarianism is by demonstrating the effectiveness of democratic governance. His administration has focused on passing legislation aimed at improving infrastructure, addressing the COVID-19 pandemic, and supporting economic recovery—measures intended to show that democracy can deliver tangible benefits for the American people.

However, this approach has been criticized for failing to address the structural issues exposed by the insurrection, including the erosion of trust in elections, the rise of political violence, and the influence of extremist ideologies within mainstream politics. By prioritizing unity over accountability, Biden's strategy risks enabling those who seek to undermine democracy to regroup and act again.

Judicial and Legislative Challenges

Biden's reliance on the judiciary and Congress to address the insurrection has faced significant obstacles:

1. **Supreme Court Inaction**: The Supreme Court has largely

avoided addressing questions related to January 6, including whether the attack constituted an insurrection under the 14th Amendment. This lack of judicial clarity has left critical constitutional questions unresolved.

2. **Congressional Investigations**: The House Select Committee on January 6 conducted a detailed investigation, producing a comprehensive report that documented Trump's role in inciting the attack and the involvement of other political figures. However, the committee's findings did not lead to concrete actions to enforce Section 3 or disqualify individuals from future office.

3. **Republican Obstruction**: The Republican Party's alignment with Trump and its efforts to downplay or justify the insurrection have hampered efforts to achieve bipartisan accountability. Republican-led state legislatures have enacted laws restricting voting access and increasing partisan control over election administration, echoing the tactics that fueled the insurrection.

Long-Term Implications

Biden's response to the insurrection has left the country at a crossroads. His decision to defer accountability to the judiciary, Congress, and the electoral process reflects a commitment to democratic norms but has also revealed the limitations of those mechanisms in addressing existential threats to democracy.

As Trump and his allies continue to exert influence, including Trump's public statements about terminating the Constitution, Biden faces a moral and constitutional dilemma. If these forces regain power, they may act on their anti-democratic agenda, undermining the very system Biden seeks to protect.

Summary of Chapter 7

President Biden's response to the insurrection has been defined by his commitment to unity, his deference to the rule of law, and his belief in the resilience of democracy. While these principles have guided his actions, they have also left critical gaps in accountability, raising questions about the long-term consequences of his approach.

As the nation grapples with the ongoing threat of authoritarianism, Biden's response will be judged not only by the success of his legislative agenda but by whether his strategy effectively safeguards democracy from future attacks. The insurrection of 2020 and its aftermath continue to shape the nation's political landscape, posing urgent questions about the balance between unity and justice.

A lingering concern with Biden's response to the insurrection by not holding the political organizers of the insurrection accountable pursuant to Section 3 of the Fourteenth Amendment is that it could not only embolden Trump and his supporters to try another insurrection, but it could encourage others on both sides of the political spectrum to use unconstitutional schemes and violence to seek and maintain governmental power.

Chapter 8: Congressional Reactions to the Insurrection

The insurrection of January 6, 2021, not only tested the resilience of American democracy but also exposed deep divisions within Congress. The legislative branch, entrusted with the constitutional responsibility of certifying the Electoral College results and upholding democratic norms, became both a target of the attack and a battlefield for competing narratives about its significance.

The responses from members of Congress to the events of January 6 and its aftermath reflected starkly contrasting views. These reactions ranged from urgent calls for accountability to efforts to downplay the attack and shield its political architects. Understanding these dynamics is critical to assessing the broader implications of the insurrection and the future of governance in the United States.

Immediate Reactions During and After the Attack

On January 6, as rioters breached the Capitol, members of Congress were forced into lockdown, with some barricaded inside chambers while others were evacuated to secure locations. The attack disrupted the joint session convened to certify the Electoral College results, delaying one of the most sacred processes in American democracy.

Bipartisan Shock and Condemnation: Initially, there was bipartisan outrage at the assault on the Capitol. Prominent Republican leaders, including Senate Majority Leader Mitch McConnell and House Minority Leader Kevin McCarthy, condemned the violence and acknowledged that the election results were legitimate. McConnell declared that the mob had been "fed lies" and that Congress would not be deterred from fulfilling its constitutional duty.

However, this moment of unity was fleeting. Within days, partisan divisions emerged as Republicans began to reframe the attack and shift blame away from Trump and his supporters.

The Impeachment of Donald Trump

In the immediate aftermath of the insurrection, the House of Representatives moved swiftly to hold Donald Trump accountable for his role in inciting the attack. On January 13, 2021, just one week after the assault, the House voted to impeach Trump for "incitement of insurrection," making him the first president in U.S. history to be impeached twice.

Key Details:

1. **H. Res. 24**: The impeachment resolution accused Trump of encouraging violence through his false claims of election fraud and his inflammatory rhetoric at the January 6 rally. The resolution passed with 232 votes, including 10 Republicans who broke ranks with their party.
2. **Senate Trial**: In February 2021, the Senate conducted Trump's second impeachment trial. Although a majority of senators—57, including 7 Republicans—voted to convict Trump, the total fell short of the two-thirds threshold required for conviction.

Impact of Impeachment Efforts: While the impeachment highlighted Trump's central role in the insurrection, his acquittal underscored the limits of congressional accountability in a polarized political environment. Republican senators who voted against conviction, including McConnell, justified their decision on procedural grounds, arguing that a former president could not be impeached—despite evidence of Trump's involvement.

The House Select Committee on January 6

In the months following the insurrection, the House of Representatives launched a formal investigation into the events of January 6 and the broader efforts to overturn the 2020 election. After initial resistance from Republican leadership to a bipartisan commission,

Speaker Nancy Pelosi established the House Select Committee on January 6 in July 2021.

Goals and Findings:

1. **Scope of Investigation**: The committee aimed to uncover the planning, coordination, and execution of the insurrection, including the roles of Trump, his allies, and extremist groups like the Oath Keepers and Proud Boys.
2. **Subpoenas and Testimony**: The committee issued hundreds of subpoenas, gathering testimony from White House officials, law enforcement, and key figures in Trump's orbit.
3. **Final Report**: In December 2022, the committee released its final report, concluding that Trump was at the center of a coordinated effort to overturn the election. The report recommended criminal charges against Trump and highlighted systemic failures in law enforcement and intelligence.

Republican Boycotts and Obstruction: Republican leaders largely boycotted the committee, with McCarthy and others dismissing it as a partisan exercise. This resistance undermined efforts to present a united front in condemning the insurrection and contributed to ongoing divisions within Congress.

The Rise of Alternative Narratives

While the House Select Committee sought to document the facts of January 6, many Republican members of Congress actively worked to rewrite the narrative of the insurrection:

1. **Downplaying the Attack**: Some Republicans characterized the rioters as "peaceful patriots" or claimed that the attack was exaggerated by the media and Democrats. Representative Andrew Clyde infamously described the events as resembling a "normal tourist visit."
2. **Deflecting Blame**: Others, including Representative Marjorie

Taylor Greene, propagated conspiracy theories suggesting that left-wing activists or federal agents had orchestrated the attack to discredit Trump supporters.

3. **Opposing Accountability**: Efforts to hold insurrectionists accountable, including prosecutions and investigations, were framed by some Republicans as "political witch hunts" designed to persecute conservatives.

Legislative Responses and Missed Opportunities

In addition to impeachment and investigative efforts, Congress had opportunities to address the systemic vulnerabilities exposed by the insurrection. However, partisan gridlock limited meaningful legislative action.

1. **Electoral Count Reform Act (2022)**: In a rare bipartisan effort, Congress passed reforms to the Electoral Count Act of 1887, clarifying the vice president's role in certifying election results as purely ceremonial and making it harder for lawmakers to object to state-certified results. While significant, this measure addressed only one aspect of the crisis.

2. **Voting Rights Legislation**: Democratic efforts to pass voting rights protections, such as the John Lewis Voting Rights Advancement Act, failed to overcome Republican opposition in the Senate. These measures aimed to counteract state-level laws restricting voting access, which were inspired by Trump's false claims of election fraud.

Partisan Implications and Political Calculations

The insurrection further deepened existing partisan divides in Congress. For Republicans, aligning with Trump and downplaying January 6 became a political litmus test, solidifying his influence over the party. For Democrats, the attack highlighted the urgent need to defend democracy, but their efforts to pursue accountability often collided with the realities of legislative math and public fatigue.

Implications for Section 3 of the 14th Amendment: Despite the clear applicability of Section 3 to Trump and certain members of Congress, there has been no effort on the part of Republican members of Congress to enforce this provision. However, the fact that Democrats and ten Republicans in the 117th Congress passed the impeachment resolution declaring Trump incited the insurrection, that along with Trump's actions, even though it did not address the actions of congressional Republicans, satisfies the self-executing aspect of Section 3, as well as Section 5, and the recommendation by the majority on the Supreme Court in Trump v. United States, that Congress needed to act in invoking Section 3 of the Fourteenth Amendment.

Summary of Chapter 8

Congress's responses to the January 6 insurrection have been a microcosm of the broader challenges facing American democracy. While some lawmakers have pursued accountability and reform, others have obstructed these efforts, perpetuating false narratives and undermining trust in democratic institutions.

The failure to fully address the root causes of the insurrection or to hold its political architects accountable has left the nation vulnerable to future crises. As Congress remains deeply divided, the question looms: Can it rise to meet the challenges of this moment, or will its inaction embolden those who seek to undermine democracy?

Chapter 9: Judicial and Institutional Obstacles

The insurrection of January 6, 2021, highlighted significant judicial and institutional failures in addressing a direct threat to the Constitution. While the judiciary, Congress, and federal agencies had tools available to enforce accountability, their responses revealed an alarming pattern: loyalty to Donald Trump among key actors appeared to supersede loyalty to the Constitution. This dynamic not only hindered efforts to address the insurrection but also exposed broader vulnerabilities in the institutional framework designed to uphold democratic norms.

Judicial Reluctance and the Role of the Supreme Court

The judiciary's response to the January 6 insurrection has been marked by a cautious and limited approach. While lower courts have addressed individual rioters and certain procedural issues, the Supreme Court has avoided substantive engagement with constitutional questions surrounding the insurrection, including the applicability of Section 3 of the 14th Amendment.

Supreme Court and Trump's Influence

My position asserts that the majority of the Supreme Court allowed loyalty to Trump—or at least deference to the political influence he commands—to guide their decisions. This influence is evident in their reluctance to engage with cases that could clarify whether January 6 constituted an insurrection under Section 3, as well as their deference to Congress to address the issue.

In **Trump v. United States**, the Court refrained from making substantive determinations about the insurrection, suggesting that Congress bore responsibility for invoking Section 3. While this deference aligns with constitutional principles of separation of powers, it also reflects the Court's apparent unwillingness to confront Trump's role in undermining the Constitution. This reluctance, whether politically motivated or rooted in judicial caution, has left critical constitutional questions unanswered by the court.

The Court's hesitancy to act has broader implications. By avoiding direct engagement with the insurrection, the judiciary has effectively deferred accountability to other branches of government, which themselves are plagued by political polarization and inaction. This deference is a violation of the oath of office for Supreme Court justices to administer the law agreeably to the Constitution and the laws of the United States.

The Self-Executing Nature of Section 3

A critical aspect of my position is that Section 3 of the 14th Amendment is self-executing. The provision's lack of a specified mechanism for enforcement is intentional, as its application hinges on the actions of "any person" who engages in insurrection or rebellion or gives aid or comfort to such actions.

Under this interpretation:

1. **The Actions Speak for Themselves**: The disqualification under Section 3 is triggered by the actions of the individual—whether through direct participation in an insurrection, incitement, or providing material support. These actions are sufficient to invoke the provision without the need for additional legislative or judicial intervention. Since Section 3 does not carry a criminal or civil conviction, due process can be sought and provided in court to determine if an insurrection occurred and if the disqualified person participated in it. If the answer to either of those questions is negative, Section 3 does not apply. Conversely, if the answer to either of those questions is affirmative, the court has no further jurisdiction, as the provision provides that only Congress, by a two-thirds vote by both houses, can dismiss the disability.

2. **Judicial Role is Limited**: Courts can determine factual

questions—whether an insurrection occurred and whether the individual participated—but they have no constitutional authority to invoke or dismiss the disqualification. This power is explicitly reserved for Congress, which may, by a two-thirds vote in each house, remove the disqualification.

By failing to engage with these principles, the judiciary has contributed to the broader institutional failure to enforce Section 3, leaving its constitutional safeguards dormant in the face of one of the most significant insurrections in American history.

Congressional Republicans and the Influence of Trump

In the aftermath of January 6, the overwhelming majority of congressional Republicans, with the notable exceptions of Representatives Liz Cheney and Adam Kinzinger, demonstrated a reluctance to hold Trump or their own members accountable. My position is that this inaction reflects their loyalty to Trump over their constitutional obligations.

Refusal to Act on Section 3

Despite the self-executing nature of Section 3, its enforcement requires political will, particularly from Congress. Republicans in Congress, however, have consistently downplayed the significance of January 6 and resisted efforts to apply Section 3 to Trump or members of their party. This reluctance is evident in:

- **The Impeachment Trial**: While 10 House Republicans voted to impeach Trump for inciting the insurrection, the majority of Republican senators voted to acquit him, despite overwhelming evidence of his role in inciting the mob.
- **Response to the House Select Committee**: Most Republican lawmakers boycotted the January 6 Committee's investigation, dismissing it as a partisan exercise rather than engaging with its findings.

- **Framing of January 6**: Many Republican members adopted rhetoric that minimized or reframed the insurrection, casting it as a legitimate protest or blaming outside actors rather than Trump or their own party.

Cheney and Kinzinger: Exceptions to the Rule

Representatives Liz Cheney and Adam Kinzinger stood apart from their party in their unwavering commitment to investigating and addressing the insurrection. As members of the House Select Committee, they were vocal in condemning Trump's actions and in supporting accountability for those involved. However, their positions made them political pariahs within their party, and both faced significant political consequences as a result.

Institutional Failures and Political Calculations

The failure to enforce Section 3 reflects broader institutional challenges that transcend any single branch of government. These challenges are rooted in systemic inertia, political calculations, and the enduring influence of Trump over key actors.

Partisan Polarization

The deep polarization within Congress has rendered it nearly impossible to achieve the bipartisan consensus necessary to address constitutional crises. Republican lawmakers, wary of alienating Trump's base, have prioritized their political survival over their constitutional responsibilities. This dynamic has left critical constitutional provisions like Section 3 unenforced, even in the face of clear evidence of their applicability.

Lack of Enforcement Mechanisms

While Section 3 is self-executing, its enforcement depends on institutional actors with the political will to act. The absence of explicit processes for applying Section 3 has allowed lawmakers and courts to avoid engaging with its implications, perpetuating a cycle of inaction.

Public Fatigue and Institutional Trust

The protracted investigations and partisan gridlock surrounding January 6 have contributed to public fatigue, undermining trust in democratic institutions. This erosion of public confidence further complicates efforts to address the systemic issues exposed by the insurrection.

Summary of Chapter 9

The judicial and institutional obstacles to enforcing accountability for the insurrection reflect a troubling dynamic: loyalty to Trump among key actors—both within Congress and the judiciary—has outweighed loyalty to the Constitution. This influence has hindered efforts to invoke Section 3 of the 14th Amendment, despite its clear applicability to Trump and certain members of Congress.

The self-executing nature of Section 3, designed to hold individuals accountable based on their actions alone, remains dormant not because of constitutional ambiguity but because of a lack of political and institutional will. As long as these obstacles persist, the nation remains vulnerable to future attacks on its democratic foundations, raising urgent questions about the resilience of American governance in the face of authoritarian threats.

Chapter 10: The Historical Use of Section 3 of the 14th Amendment

Section 3 of the 14th Amendment, ratified in 1868 during the Reconstruction Era, was created as a tool to protect the fragile Union from future threats by disqualifying those who had engaged in insurrection or rebellion against the United States. Its primary aim was to prevent former Confederates—particularly those who had previously sworn an oath to uphold the Constitution—from returning to positions of power in the government.

While Section 3 was designed with the Civil War in mind, its applicability extends to any insurrection or rebellion against the United States. Over time, its use has been sporadic and often politically charged. Examining its historical implementation offers valuable insights into its potential and limitations as a mechanism for accountability.

Origins and Initial Enforcement

Section 3 was born out of the Union's victory in the Civil War and the challenges of Reconstruction. The drafters of the 14th Amendment recognized that simply defeating the Confederacy on the battlefield was insufficient to secure the Union's long-term stability. The threat of former Confederate leaders regaining political influence posed a significant risk to the democratic ideals that the war was fought to preserve. The same challenges are relevant in the modern era in that defeating insurrectionists in a free and fair election is insufficient to secure the Union's long-term stability due to the obvious possibility that the insurrectionists who remained in the government could win the election. However, the authors of the Constitution did not leave that responsibility up to voters. Rather, in the self-executing wording of Section 3, buffered by the president's charge to take care that the laws be faithfully executed, is the constitutional prescription of how to resolve an insurrection.

Immediate Application

After the ratification of the 14th Amendment, Section 3 was enforced broadly against former Confederate officials, military officers, and politicians who had participated in the rebellion. Thousands of individuals were barred from holding federal or state office due to their roles in the Confederacy.

- **Scope of Enforcement**: The disqualification applied to anyone who had taken an oath to support the Constitution and subsequently engaged in the rebellion. This included members of Congress who had joined the Confederacy, governors of Confederate states, and military officers who had fought against the Union, as well as the former president of the Confederate, Jefferson Davis, who attempted to run for a U. S. Senate seat representing the state of Mississippi during Reconstruction but was banned from office pursuant to Section 3.
- **Challenges to Enforcement**: Enforcement of Section 3 faced resistance, particularly in the South, where many viewed it as punitive and vindictive. Some Southern states delayed ratifying the 14th Amendment, hoping to negotiate more lenient terms for reintegration into the Union.

The Amnesty Act of 1872

The broad disqualifications imposed by Section 3 proved politically contentious. By 1872, calls for reconciliation between the North and South had gained momentum, leading Congress to pass the Amnesty Act. This law removed the Section 3 disqualifications for most former Confederates, effectively granting them the ability to hold office again.

The Amnesty Act reflected a shift in national priorities from accountability to reconciliation. However, it also marked the beginning of the erosion of Reconstruction's enforcement mechanisms, as the federal government increasingly prioritized appeasing Southern leaders over protecting the rights of freed people and securing the Union's democratic foundations.

Later Uses of Section 3

After Reconstruction, Section 3 fell into disuse, its applicability largely forgotten in the context of 20th-century politics. However, it was invoked in limited and often symbolic ways in subsequent decades.

World War I and Post-War Application

In 1919, Section 3 was controversially invoked in the case of Victor L. Berger, a socialist congressman from Wisconsin. Berger, who had been convicted under the Espionage Act for opposing U.S. involvement in World War I, was denied his seat in the House of Representatives on the grounds that his actions constituted giving "aid and comfort" to the nation's enemies.

While Berger's case did not involve an insurrection, it demonstrated the potential breadth of Section 3's language. His disqualification was ultimately overturned after the Supreme Court reversed his conviction, but the case highlighted the challenges of interpreting Section 3 outside its original Reconstruction context.

Civil Rights Era and Beyond

During the Civil Rights Movement and subsequent decades, Section 3 was rarely mentioned or applied. Its perceived connection to Reconstruction and the Civil War limited its relevance in the eyes of lawmakers and courts. However, its language remained a powerful, if dormant, tool for addressing threats to the Constitution.

Modern Revivals of Section 3

The events surrounding January 6, 2021, have prompted renewed interest in Section 3 as a mechanism for accountability. While its historical use was largely confined to the Reconstruction Era, its potential relevance to contemporary challenges is undeniable.

Key Legal Challenges

Modern attempts to invoke Section 3 have focused on disqualifying individuals involved in or supporting the January 6 insurrection. These efforts have raised important questions about the provision's applicability and enforcement in the 21st century:

- **Madison Cawthorn (2022)**: Voters in North Carolina filed a legal challenge to bar Representative Madison Cawthorn from the ballot under Section 3, citing his support for the January 6 attack. The case was dismissed on procedural grounds, avoiding substantive questions about the insurrection and Cawthorn's involvement.

- **Trump's Ballot Eligibility**: Efforts to prevent Donald Trump from appearing on state ballots in future elections have invoked Section 3, arguing that his actions leading up to and during January 6 meet the criteria for disqualification. These cases remain unresolved, reflecting the judiciary's reluctance to engage with the provision's implications. In Trump v. Anderson, the Colorado Supreme Court ruled that it did not disqualify Trump pursuant to Section 3 of the Fourteenth Amendment, but rather his actions disqualified him. The court further ruled that because Section 3 disqualified Trump, the court was obligated by Colorado laws to remove him from its ballot. The U. S. Supreme Court reversed the Colorado Supreme Court's decision and ruled that states do not have the constitutional authority to enforce Section 3 of the Fourteenth Amendment. The U. S. Supreme Court refused to address whether an insurrection occurred and if Trump participated in it.

Challenges in Modern Contexts

The historical enforcement of Section 3 during Reconstruction benefited from a clear and undisputed context: the Civil War was an unequivocal rebellion against the United States. Modern applications, however, face greater ambiguity:

- **Defining "Insurrection"**: While January 6 clearly involved violent attempts to disrupt the constitutional process, those who supported the insurrection argue that it does not meet the threshold of an organized rebellion akin to the Civil War.
- **Judicial Hesitancy**: Courts have been reluctant to address the broader implications of Section 3, often focusing on procedural issues rather than engaging with the substantive questions of disqualification.
- **Political Resistance**: The polarization of modern politics has made enforcement of Section 3 politically fraught, with many Republican lawmakers dismissing its applicability to January 6.

Lessons from History

The historical use of Section 3 provides valuable insights into its potential as a tool for accountability:

1. **Self-Executing Nature**: Section 3 is self-executing, meaning that its disqualification provisions are triggered by the actions of the individual. Although Congress has a role in lifting disqualifications, the court has no role in invoking or dismissing the disqualification, but the provision itself relies on the conduct of those involved.
2. **Balancing Accountability and Reconciliation**: The Amnesty Act of 1872 demonstrates the tension between enforcing accountability and fostering national unity. Modern applications of Section 3 face similar challenges, particularly in navigating partisan divisions.

3. **Erosion of Enforcement Mechanisms**: The decline of Section 3's use after Reconstruction underscores the importance of political will in enforcing constitutional provisions. Without sustained commitment, even the most robust safeguards can become dormant.

Summary of Chapter 10

Section 3 of the 14th Amendment was a vital tool for safeguarding the Union during Reconstruction, ensuring that those who had betrayed the Constitution could not regain power. Its historical use reveals both its potential and its limitations as a mechanism for accountability.

While the provision has been largely dormant for much of its history, the events of January 6 have demonstrated its enduring relevance. However, its enforcement in modern contexts depends on overcoming significant judicial and institutional obstacles, as well as mustering the political will to prioritize the Constitution over partisan loyalties.

The lessons of history remind us that constitutional tools like Section 3 are only as effective as the institutions and leaders entrusted with their application. The challenge today is whether these institutions can rise to meet the moment, ensuring that the mistakes of the past are not repeated.

Chapter 11: The Amnesty Act of 1872 and Its Long-Term Implications

The Amnesty Act of 1872 marked a pivotal moment in American history, significantly influencing the trajectory of Reconstruction and the subsequent establishment of Jim Crow laws. By lifting the disqualifications imposed by Section 3 of the 14th Amendment on most former Confederates, the Act facilitated their reintegration into political life. This chapter examines how the Amnesty Act contributed to the premature end of Reconstruction, the rise of Jim Crow laws, and the delayed progress toward equality for African Americans and women until the 1960s. Additionally, it explores the dormancy of Section 3 in the absence of events comparable to the Civil War until the insurrection incited by former President Trump.

Impact of the Amnesty Act on Reconstruction and the Rise of Jim Crow

The Amnesty Act of 1872 removed political disabilities from most individuals who had participated in the Confederacy, allowing them to hold public office and vote. This legislative shift had profound consequences for the Reconstruction era and the subsequent establishment of systemic racial segregation.

Premature Conclusion of Reconstruction

By restoring political rights to former Confederates, the Amnesty Act undermined the efforts of Reconstruction to transform Southern society and protect the rights of newly freed African Americans. The reintegration of former Confederates into political power led to:

- **Erosion of Federal Enforcement**: With former Confederates regaining influence, there was a concerted effort to dismantle Reconstruction policies and reduce federal oversight in the South. This shift allowed for the resurgence of pre-war power structures and the suppression of African American rights.

- **Suppression of African American Political Participation**: The return of former Confederates to political office resulted in the implementation of measures aimed at disenfranchising African American voters and curtailing their political representation.

Establishment of Jim Crow Laws

The empowerment of former Confederates facilitated the creation of Jim Crow laws, which institutionalized racial segregation and discrimination. These laws:

- **Legalized Racial Segregation**: Enforced separation in public facilities, education, and transportation, relegating African Americans to inferior conditions.
- **Disenfranchised African Americans**: Through mechanisms such as literacy tests, poll taxes, and grandfather clauses, African Americans were systematically denied the right to vote.

Delayed Progress Toward Equality

The consequences of the Amnesty Act extended beyond the immediate post-Reconstruction era, delaying progress toward equality for African Americans and women until the civil rights movements of the 1960s.

Impact on African Americans

The resurgence of white supremacist power structures and the entrenchment of Jim Crow laws resulted in:

- **Economic Disparities**: Limited access to quality education and employment opportunities perpetuated cycles of poverty within African American communities.
- **Social Marginalization**: Segregation and discriminatory

practices reinforced societal norms that devalued African American lives and contributions.

Impact on Women

While the Amnesty Act primarily affected racial dynamics, the broader societal regression it facilitated also impeded progress for women's rights:

- **Stagnation of Women's Suffrage**: The focus on racial issues and the suppression of African American rights diverted attention and resources from the women's suffrage movement, delaying the passage of the 19th Amendment until 1920.
- **Perpetuation of Gender Inequality**: The reinforcement of conservative social norms hindered efforts to address gender disparities in education, employment, and legal rights.

Dormancy of Section 3 and Its Modern Relevance

Since the Civil War, Section 3 of the 14th Amendment has remained largely dormant, primarily because the nation had not experienced an event comparable to the Civil War until the insurrection incited by former President Trump.

Historical Dormancy

The absence of large-scale insurrections or rebellions against the United States government contributed to the infrequent invocation of Section 3. Its application was largely limited to the immediate post-Civil War period, with few instances of enforcement in subsequent decades.

Modern Relevance

The events of January 6, 2021, where a violent mob stormed the U.S. Capitol in an attempt to overturn the presidential election results, have renewed interest in Section 3. The insurrection, incited by former President Trump, who had taken an oath to support the Constitution, raises questions about the applicability of Section 3 in holding accountable those who engage in or support insurrectionist activities.

Summary of Chapter 11

The Amnesty Act of 1872 played a significant role in ending the Reconstruction era and establishing the Jim Crow laws, delaying progress toward equality for African Americans and women until the civil rights movements of the 1960s. The dormancy of Section 3 since the Civil War reflects the absence of comparable insurrectionist events until the recent past. Understanding this history is crucial in evaluating the tools available to protect and preserve democratic institutions in the face of contemporary challenges.

Chapter 12: Modern Challenges in Enforcing Section 3 of the 14th Amendment

The events of January 6, 2021, have reignited discussions about the applicability and enforcement of Section 3 of the 14th Amendment, which disqualifies individuals who have engaged in insurrection from holding public office. While this provision was primarily utilized during the Reconstruction era, its relevance in contemporary contexts presents several challenges.

Defining "Insurrection" in the Modern Era

A central challenge lies in interpreting what constitutes an "insurrection" under Section 3. The term is not explicitly defined within the Constitution, leading to debates over its application to events like the January 6 attack on the U.S. Capitol.

- **Historical Context**: Historically, "insurrection" referred to organized efforts to overthrow or undermine the government, as seen during the Civil War.
- **Contemporary Interpretation**: Applying this term to modern events requires careful consideration of the scale, organization, and intent behind actions challenging governmental authority.

Judicial Reluctance and Legal Ambiguities

The judiciary has shown hesitancy in addressing cases related to Section 3, often citing procedural grounds or deferring to other branches of government.

- **Case Examples:**
    - *Cawthorn v. Amalfi*: The U.S. Court of Appeals for the Fourth Circuit found that the Amnesty Act of 1872 does not apply to

later insurrections or treasonous acts, indicating that Section 3 could still be relevant today.

Congressional Research Service[1]

- *Trump v. Anderson*: The Colorado Supreme Court ruled that former President Trump's actions disqualified him under Section 3, but the U.S. Supreme Court reversed this decision, stating that states do not have the constitutional authority to enforce Section 3.

National Constitution Center[2]

- **Legal Ambiguities**: The lack of clear definitions and precedents complicates judicial decisions, leading to inconsistent applications of Section 3.

Political Polarization and Enforcement Challenges

The enforcement of Section 3 is further complicated by deep political divisions.

- **Partisan Interpretations**: Political affiliations often influence perspectives on what constitutes insurrection and who should be held accountable.
- **Legislative Inaction**: Congress has the authority to enforce Section 3, but partisan gridlock has impeded efforts to apply this provision to contemporary cases.

Institutional Mechanisms and Procedural Hurdles

1. https://crsreports.congress.gov/product/pdf/lsb/lsb10569

2. https://constitutioncenter.org/blog/explaining-donald-trumps-14th-amendment-case-at-the-supreme-court

Implementing Section 3 requires clear procedures and institutional commitment.

- **Lack of Established Processes**: There is no standardized mechanism for determining disqualification under Section 3, leading to ad hoc approaches.
- **Due Process Considerations**: Ensuring fair procedures for those accused of insurrection is essential to uphold constitutional rights.

Public Perception and the Role of Media

Media coverage and public opinion play significant roles in shaping the discourse around Section 3.

- **Media Influence**: Media narratives can sway public perception, either supporting or undermining efforts to enforce Section 3.
- **Public Awareness**: Educating the public about the provisions and implications of Section 3 is crucial for informed civic engagement.

Summary of Chapter 12

Enforcing Section 3 of the 14th Amendment in the modern era presents multifaceted challenges, including definitional ambiguities, judicial reluctance, political polarization, procedural hurdles, and the influence of media and public perception. Addressing these challenges requires a concerted effort across all branches of government and society to uphold constitutional principles and ensure accountability for actions that threaten democratic institutions.

Chapter 13: Lincoln and Biden: A Comparison of Actions and Inactions

The United States has faced existential threats to its democratic foundation twice in its history—first during Abraham Lincoln's presidency amid the secession of the Confederate states and the Civil War, and again during Joe Biden's presidency in the wake of the January 6, 2021, insurrection. Both leaders found themselves at the helm during crises that tested the resilience of the Union, and their responses provide compelling insights into the challenges of leadership when democracy itself is at stake.

While Lincoln and Biden faced vastly different historical and political contexts, their decisions—or lack thereof—illuminate how leaders navigate the tension between enforcing the rule of law, preserving the nation's unity, and balancing political considerations.

Lincoln's Response to Secession

From the outset of his presidency, Abraham Lincoln faced the secession of Southern states following his election in 1860. These states, driven by the preservation of slavery, declared their independence to form the Confederate States of America. Lincoln's approach to the crisis was defined by three core principles:

1. **The Indivisibility of the Union**: Lincoln maintained that the Union was perpetual, and that secession was unconstitutional. In his inaugural address, he appealed to the shared history and values of the nation, stating that the Union must be preserved at all costs.

2. **Strategic Restraint**: Lincoln initially avoided aggressive measures to bring seceding states back into the Union, fearing that such actions might alienate Border States or escalate the conflict prematurely. His decision to resupply Fort Sumter was

a calculated move to provoke Confederate forces into firing the first shot, thereby unifying the North around the need for war.

3. **Decisive Action Once War Began**: After the Confederacy's attack on Fort Sumter, Lincoln moved swiftly to mobilize the Union's resources, calling for volunteers and issuing orders to blockade Southern ports. His Emancipation Proclamation reframed the war as a moral fight against slavery, strengthening the Union's resolve and undercutting Confederate legitimacy.

Lincoln balanced a delicate line between reconciliation and accountability. His policies during and after the war sought to reintegrate the South without compromising the Union's principles or granting impunity to Confederate leaders. While he supported efforts to prevent insurrectionists from regaining political power, Lincoln's ultimate goal was to rebuild the nation, even at the expense of punitive measures.

Biden's Response to Insurrection

President Joe Biden faced a markedly different crisis in January 2021. The attack on the U.S. Capitol by supporters of outgoing President Donald Trump sought to overturn the results of the 2020 presidential election and disrupt the peaceful transfer of power. Biden's response to this crisis was shaped by his commitment to constitutional democracy and his vision of national unity:

1. **Condemnation of Insurrection**: Biden repeatedly condemned the January 6 attack as an assault on democracy, framing it as a stark moment in the nation's history. He emphasized the importance of protecting the Constitution and upholding the rule of law.

2. **Deferral to the Electoral Process**: Rather than invoking Section 3 of the 14th Amendment or advocating for aggressive

legal action against those involved in the insurrection, Biden focused on letting the electoral process play out. He framed his presidency as an opportunity for Americans to choose between democracy and authoritarianism through future elections.

3. **Refraining from Constitutional Enforcement**: Despite significant evidence, including the findings of the House Select Committee on January 6 and **H. Res. 24 (117th Congress)**—which declared that Trump incited an insurrection—Biden did not pursue Section 3 disqualifications against Trump or other Republican members of Congress who supported the insurrection. His administration's approach prioritized unity over enforcement of constitutional provisions.

Biden's inaction on Section 3 has drawn criticism for failing to hold insurrectionists accountable and allowing anti-democratic forces to persist within government institutions. While his approach sought to avoid deepening political divisions, it has raised questions about the long-term implications for constitutional governance.

Similarities Between Lincoln and Biden

Both Lincoln and Biden faced crises that tested the integrity of the United States, and their responses share several parallels:

1. **Emphasis on Unity**: Both leaders prioritized preserving the nation over punitive measures. Lincoln sought to reintegrate the South without alienating its people, while Biden emphasized reconciliation and healing, avoiding actions that might deepen the country's partisan divide.

2. **Navigating Political Constraints**: Lincoln had to contend with the divided loyalties of Border States and a Northern populace initially reluctant to wage war. Similarly, Biden faced a polarized electorate, and a Republican Party increasingly

aligned with Trump's authoritarian rhetoric.

3. **Efforts to Uphold Democratic Principles**: Both presidents framed their actions within the context of protecting democracy. Lincoln tied the Union's survival to the broader fight against slavery, while Biden highlighted the stakes of preserving constitutional democracy against authoritarian threats.

Key Differences in Approach

While their contexts were different, the divergence in Lincoln and Biden's actions highlights critical distinctions in their leadership:

1. **Decisive Enforcement vs. Deferral**: Lincoln's decision to resupply Fort Sumter and later issue the Emancipation Proclamation demonstrated a willingness to act decisively, even when such actions carried political risks. In contrast, Biden deferred constitutional enforcement of Section 3, opting instead to allow voters to determine the nation's future through elections.

2. **Accountability for Insurrectionists**: Lincoln's policies during Reconstruction included mechanisms to disqualify Confederate leaders from holding office, reflecting a commitment to accountability. Biden, however, refrained from enforcing Section 3 against Trump or Republican members of Congress who supported the insurrection, effectively leaving their disqualification unaddressed.

3. **Direct Confrontation vs. Strategic Avoidance**: Lincoln directly confronted the secessionist states, recognizing that preserving the Union required military and legal action. Biden's reluctance to engage with Section 3 or challenge the Supreme Court's inaction reflected a more cautious approach, potentially undermining constitutional safeguards.

Constitutional Duty and Leadership

From my perspective, Biden's decision not to enforce Section 3 represents a failure to fulfill his constitutional duty. While Lincoln's leadership was defined by his willingness to make difficult choices to preserve the Union, Biden's inaction has allowed insurrectionists to retain power and threaten the Constitution's future.

This raises critical questions about the role of the presidency in defending constitutional democracy. Is it sufficient for a president to rely on elections to resolve existential crises, or does the oath of office require proactive enforcement of constitutional provisions? In Biden's case, allowing a potential transfer of power to a president-elect who has expressed intent to terminate the Constitution would appear to violate his duty to "preserve, protect, and defend" the nation's foundational principles.

Summary of Chapter 13

The crises faced by Lincoln and Biden offer valuable lessons about leadership in moments of profound national peril. While both presidents sought to navigate the challenges of division and insurrection, their approaches reveal differing commitments to accountability and constitutional enforcement.

Lincoln's decisive actions ensured that the Union's survival was not left to chance, even as he sought reconciliation. In contrast, Biden's deference to electoral outcomes risks emboldening forces that threaten democracy. As the nation continues to grapple with the legacy of January 6, 2021, and the ongoing erosion of democratic norms, the choices of its leaders will determine whether the Constitution remains a living, enforceable document or becomes a relic of unfulfilled promises.

Sources

Encyclopedia Britannica[1]
Secession | History, Definition, Crisis, & Facts | Britannica[2]
October 6, 2024 — Secession, the withdrawal of 11 slave states (states in which slaveholding was legal) from the Union during 1860–61 following the election of Abraham Lincoln as president of the United States. The sec...[3]

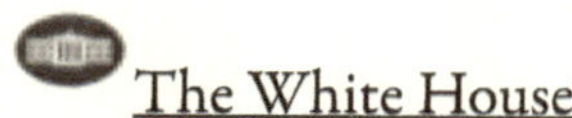The White House[4]
Remarks by President Biden on the Third Anniversary of the January 6th ...[5]
January 5, 2024 — And it's not winning because of Joe Biden. It's winning. This is the first national election since January 6th insurrection placed a dagger at the throat of American democracy — since that ...[6]

---

1. https://www.britannica.com/topic/secession

2.   **https://www.britannica.com/topic/secession**

3.   https://www.britannica.com/topic/secession

4. https://www.whitehouse.gov/briefing-room/speeches-remarks/2024/01/05/remarks-by-president-biden-on-the-third-anniversary-of-the-january-6th-attack-and-defending-the-sacred-cause-of-american-democracy-blue-bell-pa/

5.   **https://www.whitehouse.gov/briefing-room/speeches-remarks/2024/01/05/remarks-by-president-biden-on-the-third-anniversary-of-the-january-6th-attack-and-defending-the-sacred-cause-of-american-democracy-blue-bell-pa/**

6.   https://www.whitehouse.gov/briefing-room/speeches-remarks/2024/01/05/remarks-by-president-biden-on-the-third-anniversary-of-the-january-6th-attack-and-defending-the-sacred-cause-of-american-democracy-blue-bell-pa/

PBS[7]

WATCH: Biden lambastes Trump for Jan. 6 Capitol riot, a day 'we … - PBS[8]

January 4, 2024 — Federal appeals court rules Trump can be sued for inciting violence on Jan. 6. By Alanna Durkin Richer, Associated Press. Go Deeper. capitol insurrection; donald trump news; jan 6; joe biden …[9]

CNN[10]

'Trump did nothing': Biden reflects on January 6 insurrection[11]
January 4, 2024 — President Joe Biden called out Trump for refusing to condemn political violence as he opened his 2024 campaign push with a speech in Pennsylvania. … Biden reflects on January 6 insurrection [12] …

CBS News[13]

---

7. https://www.pbs.org/newshour/politics/watch-live-biden-marks-jan-6-anniversary-with-campaign-speech-on-sacred-cause-of-democracy

8. **https://www.pbs.org/newshour/politics/watch-live-biden-marks-jan-6-anniversary-with-campaign-speech-on-sacred-cause-of-democracy**

9. https://www.pbs.org/newshour/politics/watch-live-biden-marks-jan-6-anniversary-with-campaign-speech-on-sacred-cause-of-democracy

10. https://www.cnn.com/videos/politics/2024/01/05/biden-speech-democracry-trump-sot-vpx.cnn

11. **https://www.cnn.com/videos/politics/2024/01/05/biden-speech-democracry-trump-sot-vpx.cnn**

12. https://www.cnn.com/videos/politics/2024/01/05/biden-speech-democracry-trump-sot-vpx.cnn

13. https://www.cbsnews.com/live-updates/january-6-aniversary-biden-democracy-capitol-riot/

Biden denounces Trump's "web of lies" while Congress marks one year ...[14]

January 7, 2022 — Washington — President Biden marked one year since the January 6 assault on the U.S. Capitol with a fiery speech at the site of the insurrection, rebuking the violence and former President ...[15]

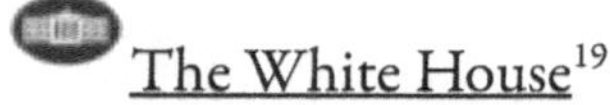NPR[16]

Live updates: Jan. 6 insurrection anniversary events | NPR[17]

January 6, 2022 — Live updates: The nation remembers the Jan. 6 insurrection. Vice President Harris and President Biden arrive to give remarks at the U.S. Capitol on Jan. 6. It has been a year since pro-Trump ...[18]

The White House[19]

Remarks By President Biden To Mark One Year Since The January 6th ...[20]

---

14.   https://www.cbsnews.com/live-updates/january-6-aniversary-biden-democracy-capitol-riot/

15.   https://www.cbsnews.com/live-updates/january-6-aniversary-biden-democracy-capitol-riot/

16. https://www.npr.org/live-updates/jan-6-anniversary-events

17.   https://www.npr.org/live-updates/jan-6-anniversary-events

18.   https://www.npr.org/live-updates/jan-6-anniversary-events

19. https://www.whitehouse.gov/briefing-room/speeches-remarks/2022/01/06/remarks-by-president-biden-to-mark-one-year-since-the-january-6th-deadly-assault-on-the-u-s-capitol/

20.   https://www.whitehouse.gov/briefing-room/speeches-remarks/2022/01/06/remarks-by-president-biden-to-mark-one-year-since-the-january-6th-deadly-assault-on-the-u-s-capitol/

<u>January 5, 2022 — U.S. CapitolWashington, D.C. 9:16 A.M. EST THE PRESIDENT: Madam Vice President, my fellow Americans: To state the obvious, one year ago today, in[21]</u>

PBS[22]

<u>WATCH: 'Democracy was attacked' during Jan. 6 insurrection, Biden says ...[23]</u>

<u>January 5, 2022 — As Biden is prepared to direct blame toward the former president, the percentage of Americans who blame Trump for the Jan. 6 riot has grown slightly over the past year, with 57% saying he bears [24] ...</u>

CNN[25]

<u>Live updates: The January 6 Capitol insurrection one-year anniversary ...[26]</u>

---

21.   https://www.whitehouse.gov/briefing-room/speeches-remarks/2022/01/06/remarks-by-president-biden-to-mark-one-year-since-the-january-6th-deadly-assault-on-the-u-s-capitol/

22. https://www.pbs.org/newshour/politics/watch-live-biden-harris-mark-anniversary-of-of-jan-6-capitol-riot

23.   **https://www.pbs.org/newshour/politics/watch-live-biden-harris-mark-anniversary-of-of-jan-6-capitol-riot**

24.   https://www.pbs.org/newshour/politics/watch-live-biden-harris-mark-anniversary-of-of-jan-6-capitol-riot

25. https://edition.cnn.com/politics/live-news/january-6-capitol-insurrection-anniversary/h_61e6f759c9f191d20cf38788e05355f0/

26.   **https://edition.cnn.com/politics/live-news/january-6-capitol-insurrection-anniversary/h_61e6f759c9f191d20cf38788e05355f0/**

January 5, 2022 — Members of Congress and President Biden are marking the one-year anniversary of the deadly Jan. 6 attack on the Capitol with a slate of commemorative events. Follow here for the latest news.[27]

CNN[28]

Watch President Biden's entire January 6th speech - CNN[29]

January 5, 2022 — President Joe Biden marked the first anniversary of the January 6 insurrection by forcefully calling out former President Donald Trump for attempting to undo American democracy, saying such an ...[30]

CBS News[31]

January 6th Capitol assault: 60 Minutes reporting - CBS News[32]

January 5, 2022 — The Threat (January 17, 2021) 13:32 On January 6, 2021, thousands of pro-Trump demonstrators marched on the Capitol, trying to stop the vote count that confirmed Joe Biden's electoral college win.[33]

---

27.   https://edition.cnn.com/politics/live-news/january-6-capitol-insurrection-anniversary/h_61e6f759c9f191d20cf38788e05355f0/

28. https://www.cnn.com/videos/politics/2022/01/06/joe-biden-entire-january-6th-speech-sot-seo.cnn

29.   **https://www.cnn.com/videos/politics/2022/01/06/joe-biden-entire-january-6th-speech-sot-seo.cnn**

30.   https://www.cnn.com/videos/politics/2022/01/06/joe-biden-entire-january-6th-speech-sot-seo.cnn

31. https://www.cbsnews.com/news/january-6-capitol-assault-60-minutes/

32.   **https://www.cbsnews.com/news/january-6-capitol-assault-60-minutes/**

ThoughtCo[34]

Order of Secession During the American Civil War - ThoughtCo[35]

May 29, 2019 — The Civil War had many causes, and Lincoln's election on Nov. 6, 1860, made many in the South feel that their cause was never going to be heard. ... The Men of Secession and Civil War, 1859-1861. The...[36]

NEH-Edsitement[37]

Lesson 2: The First Inaugural Address (1861)—Defending the American ...[38]

February 8, 2018 — Abraham Lincoln felt that the attempt of seven states to leave the American union peacefully was, in fact, a total violation of law and order. This lesson will examine Lincoln's First Inaugural Addres...[39]

33.   https://www.cbsnews.com/news/january-6-capitol-assault-60-minutes/

34. https://www.thoughtco.com/order-of-secession-during-civil-war-104535

35.   https://www.thoughtco.com/order-of-secession-during-civil-war-104535

36.   https://www.thoughtco.com/order-of-secession-during-civil-war-104535

37. https://edsitement.neh.gov/lesson-plans/lesson-2-first-inaugural-address-1861-defending-american-union

38.   https://edsitement.neh.gov/lesson-plans/lesson-2-first-inaugural-address-1861-defending-american-union

39.   https://edsitement.neh.gov/lesson-plans/lesson-2-first-inaugural-address-1861-defending-american-union

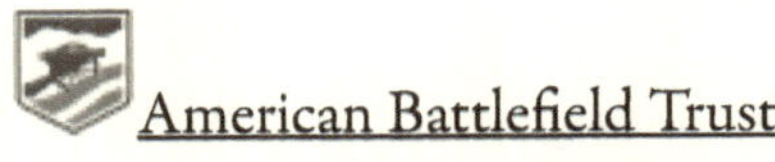American Battlefield Trust[40]

The Gathering Storm: The Secession Crisis - American Battlefield Trust[41]

April 3, 2017 — The Election of 1860. In 1860, Abraham Lincoln completed his rise from relative obscurity by capturing the Republican Party's nomination for president. His skill as an orator had captivated the North....[42]

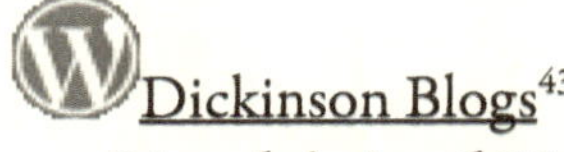Dickinson Blogs[43]

Lincoln's April 15, 1861 Presidential Proclamation[44]

April 27, 2015 — At the time of the proclamation the Secession Convention of Virginia was meeting in Richmond. [10] ... Lincoln's call for southerners to return to their homes was unheeded as the southern ranks were b...[45]

NPS.gov[46]

40. https://www.battlefields.org/learn/articles/gathering-storm-secession-crisis

41.   https://www.battlefields.org/learn/articles/gathering-storm-secession-crisis

42.   https://www.battlefields.org/learn/articles/gathering-storm-secession-crisis

43. https://blogs.dickinson.edu/hist-288pinsker/2015/04/28/lincolns-april-15-1861-presidential-proclamation/

44.   https://blogs.dickinson.edu/hist-288pinsker/2015/04/28/lincolns-april-15-1861-presidential-proclamation/

45.   https://blogs.dickinson.edu/hist-288pinsker/2015/04/28/lincolns-april-15-1861-presidential-proclamation/

46. https://www.nps.gov/liho/learn/historyculture/secessiontableofcontents.htm

Lincoln on Secession - Lincoln Home National Historic Site (U.S ...[47]

April 9, 2015 — 2. Secession is unlawful. 3. A government that allows secession will disintegrate into anarchy. 4. That Americans are not enemies, but friends. 5. Secession would destroy the world's only existing dem...[48]

 NPS.gov[49]

Secession: Why Lincoln Feared it was the End of Democracy[50]

Lincoln understood this well, so when he described America as "the world's last best hope," the words were not idle ones. Lincoln truly believed that if the Civil War was lost, it would not only have...[51]

 NEH-Edsitement[52]

Lincoln Goes to War - NEH-Edsitement[53]

Activity 1. Review events that led up to Battle at Fort Sumter. The Battle of Fort Sumter, though one of the shortest of the Civil War and one of the few with no casualties on either side, remains a k...[54]

47.   https://www.nps.gov/liho/learn/historyculture/secessiontableofcontents.htm

48.   https://www.nps.gov/liho/learn/historyculture/secessiontableofcontents.htm

49. https://www.nps.gov/articles/secession-why-lincoln-feared-it-was-the-end-of-democracy.htm

50.   https://www.nps.gov/articles/secession-why-lincoln-feared-it-was-the-end-of-democracy.htm

51.   https://www.nps.gov/articles/secession-why-lincoln-feared-it-was-the-end-of-democracy.htm

52. https://edsitement.neh.gov/lesson-plans/lincoln-goes-war

53.   https://edsitement.neh.gov/lesson-plans/lincoln-goes-war

54.   https://edsitement.neh.gov/lesson-plans/lincoln-goes-war

Miller Center[55]
July 4, 1861: July 4th Message to Congress - Miller Center[56]
Between the fall of Fort Sumter on April 13, 1861, and July of that same year, President Lincoln took a number of actions in response to secession without Congressional approval. In this special messa...[57]

Digital History[58]
Digital History - University of Houston[59]
In this way, Lincoln hoped to make the Confederacy responsible for starting a war. Upon learning of Lincoln's plan, Jefferson Davis ordered General Pierre G.T. Beauregard (1818-1893) to force Fort Sum...[60]

W Wikipedia[61]
January 6 United States Capitol attack - Wikipedia[62]
Insurrection suppressed; The deaths of six people [a]; Assaults on at least 174 police officers [16]; Delay of counting electoral votes by several hours [17]; Extensive physical damage; [7] [18] [19]...[63]

---

55. https://millercenter.org/the-presidency/presidential-speeches/july-4-1861-july-4th-message-congress

56.   https://millercenter.org/the-presidency/presidential-speeches/july-4-1861-july-4th-message-congress

57.   https://millercenter.org/the-presidency/presidential-speeches/july-4-1861-july-4th-message-congress

58. https://www.digitalhistory.uh.edu/disp_textbook.cfm?psid=3059&smtID=2

59.   https://www.digitalhistory.uh.edu/disp_textbook.cfm?psid=3059&smtID=2

60.   https://www.digitalhistory.uh.edu/disp_textbook.cfm?psid=3059&smtID=2

61. https://en.wikipedia.org/wiki/January_6_United_States_Capitol_attack

62.   https://en.wikipedia.org/wiki/January_6_United_States_Capitol_attack

University of Chicago Press[64]

Lincoln's Constitution: an interview with Daniel Farber[65]

In Lincoln's Constitution, Farber examines the greatest constitutional crisis in American history—state secession and civil war—and explores the legality of Lincoln's response to it. From his deft ana...[66]

Civil War on the Western Border[67]

Lincoln, Abraham - Civil War on the Western Border[68]

Slavery was the leading issue and the ordinances of secession from the newly formed Confederate states document that the South saw the protection and expansion of slavery as the locus of its rebellion...[69]

CNN[70]

January 6 insurrection at the US Capitol - CNN International[71]

Coverage of the January 6, 2021, insurrection at the US Capitol building. Read articles and watch videos[72]

---

63.   https://en.wikipedia.org/wiki/January_6_United_States_Capitol_attack

64. https://press.uchicago.edu/Misc/Chicago/237931in.html

65.   https://press.uchicago.edu/Misc/Chicago/237931in.html

66.   https://press.uchicago.edu/Misc/Chicago/237931in.html

67. https://civilwaronthewesternborder.org/encyclopedia/lincoln-abraham

68.   https://civilwaronthewesternborder.org/encyclopedia/lincoln-abraham

69.   https://civilwaronthewesternborder.org/encyclopedia/lincoln-abraham

70. https://edition.cnn.com/politics/january-6-insurrection

71.   https://edition.cnn.com/politics/january-6-insurrection

72.   https://edition.cnn.com/politics/january-6-insurrection